A play based on the Gospel of John

THE WORD THAT CHANGED THE WORLD

TONY BOWER

Kevin
Mayhew

First published in 2001 by
KEVIN MAYHEW LTD
Buxhall, Stowmarket, Suffolk IP14 3BW
Email: info@kevinmayhewltd.com

9 8 7 6 5 4 3 2 1 0

ISBN 1 84003 781 4
Catalogue Number 1500447

Cover design by Jonathan Stroulger
Edited and typeset by Elisabeth Bates

Printed in Great Britain

CONTENTS

ABOUT THE AUTHOR

Tony Bower is married to Claire with one son, Joseph. He has been a Christian Schools' Worker for over eight years. This is his second book, being the one that came after his first book. Tony is an able mathematician but hopefully a better writer. Having bought this book I hope you agree. Remember Tony is counting on you, as long as there are no more than ten of you.

A WORD OF THANKS . . .

. . . to Julian Lailey who had the faith to put this play on in his school; to Charles Price for commissioning Capernwray students to perform their production of the play. To Kate and Debbie for all their hard work in typing, retyping and having the ability to read my handwriting; hope my spelling kept you amused. To Pete for his musical arrangements and discerning the notes I always failed to reach! To Phil and his expertise on the music score. To Claire and her sister Jill for baking the best cakes on the planet (was that a good enough plug for 'Just Cakes'?). To all the coffee shops I frequent, a constant source of . . . coffee and space to write. To Barnsley FC for always being there for my dad and brother. Remember, Barnsley FC, they're there for you too.

INTRODUCTION

The Word that Changed the World was an idea conceived in 1999 from a desire to present the amazing life story of Jesus Christ – the Word who continues to change the world in the third millennium.

The play is based on the Gospel of John. An official and a soldier look at a report on the life of Jesus shortly after the resurrection has taken place. These two characters link each scene. The dramatic licence taken is in imagining what might have happened before or after an encounter with Jesus, i.e. What might the waiters at the wedding have said before the miracle took place? What might Nicodemus have been thinking after Jesus said, 'You must be born again'?

Throughout the performance the play helps to build a powerful picture of who Jesus is and blow away the myths that surround the resurrection.

The play was first performed by four schools at Ripley St. Thomas in Lancaster. Since its birth the play has continued to grow and was performed by an international group of students at Capernwray Hall, Carnforth, in December 2000. Both productions contained the words of the script but had some differences. The different approaches worked and both sets of performances were a huge success.

In the school production the play began with an up-tempo dance number following the narrator's reading of the passage, 'In the beginning was the word . . .' The dance depicted the creation, and with the combination of music, movement and colourful banners, went down a storm.

In the Capernwray production the play began with a choral group singing a beautiful piece of music focused on the Word becoming flesh. To start the wedding scene they began with a ceilidh which worked well and created a dramatic impact at the start of the play.

I share these items to show the flexibility that is possible with the play and also to show that it is good for each individual group to bring their own gifts and talents to the production.

The script works extremely well as it stands and because of the way it has been written can be performed very simply, i.e. with few props and simple costume. The scenes can be played with the amount of key characters scripted but can also take additional actors as and where necessary. The wedding scene benefits from having party guests on stage before the speaking begins to create an atmosphere and portray the picture of what is going on. The blind man in the court scene with the Pharisee also lends itself to a cast being added as a kind of public gallery to the drama. Once again the key word is 'flexibility'. If the play is being performed on a large stage then it is good, when possible, to 'fill' the stage. If the play is performed in a smaller venue then other practicalities may take precedence.

There is an alternative to using the song 'Tonight' if you wish to use the play without any music. The scene is a key element in showing the cross and the sacrificial love of Jesus (whether you use a song or not). The song 'Alpha and Omega' can be used as a finale. It is an up-tempo number musically and lyrically shows various facets of who Jesus is. By having the possibility of using songs (or dance) as well as being performed purely as a play the 'Word' is, I hope, being made available and accessible to a wide range of groups.

I pray that your group will have a wonderful time rehearsing and performing the play, in sharing the Word who is still active in changing our world.

Tony Bower
January 2001

CAST

Narrator 1	Man
Narrator 2	Woman
Narrator 3	Harry
Official	Larry
Soldier	Healed blind man
Waiter 1	Pharisee
Waiter 2	Mary
Wedding guests	Martha
Mary	Shop assistants x2
Nicodemus	Woman
Joseph	Manager
Women at the well x3	James
Samaritan woman	Salome
Crowd of people	Peter
Healed cripple	John
Pharisee	

Although there are two Pharisees listed, it could be the same Pharisee in the two separate scenes.

There could be additional extras added to the courtroom scene if required.

PROPS

PA system
Spotlights
Desk, chair and candle for Official and Soldier
Jugs and glasses (optional) for the feast
Mat for 'See how they leap'
Paper contracts for 'Using your loaf'
Baskets and clothes for 'Well, well . . .'

There are very few props required to perform this play. Most actions can be mimed, most props imagined. Alternatively you may prefer to provide items for individual scenes. The scenes will flow if there is minimal movement of equipment and props involved.

COSTUME

Costume is very much a matter of personal choice. Simple colourful T-shirts can work effectively or alternatively you may wish every character to dress in authentic costumes. Having a strong outfit for the Soldier and Official does help to lift their characters as central figures who link every scene.

STAGING

The main stage is the venue for all the ten different scenes. The Soldier and Official are based at one side of the stage. They are in view all the time and therefore need to 'freeze' whilst the action switches to the main stage. A spotlight fixed on the two link characters will make life easy and help to move the audience's attention, i.e. lights down on main stage after scene finishes, lights up on Soldier and Official. It is very simple and an effective way of changing scenes.

PROLOGUE

The stage is set in darkness. Off-stage (this could be prerecorded if possible and played over the PA) an actor speaks:

Narrator 1   In the beginning

> *The second and third narrators need to speak as an echo, to create an atmosphere and add depth to what is being said.*

Narrator 2   the beginning

Narrator 3   the beginning

Narrator 1   was the Word

Narrator 2   the Word

Narrator 3   the Word

Narrator 1   and the Word was with God

Narrator 2   with God

Narrator 3   with God

Narrator 1   and the Word was God

Narrator 2   was God

Narrator 3   was God

Narrator 1   He was with God

Narrator 2   with God

Narrator 3   with God

Narrator 1   in the beginning

Narrator 2   the beginning

Narrator 3   the beginning

Narrator 1   through him

Narrator 2   through him

Narrator 3   through him

Narrator 1   all things were made

Narrator 2   were made

Narrator 3   were made

Narrator 1   In him was life

Narrator 2   was life

Narrator 3   was life

Narrator 1   and that life was the light of men

Narrator 2   the light

Narrator 3   the light

Narrator 1   The light shines in the darkness

Narrator 2   the light shines

Narrator 3   the light shines

On the line 'The light shines' spotlights hit the stage.

Narrator 1   but the darkness has not overcome it

Narrator 2   not overcome

Narrator 3   not overcome

More lights on stage

Narrator 1   The Word

Narrator 2   the Word

Narrator 3   the Word

Narrator 1   became . . .

A cry of a baby is heard

Narrator 2   flesh

THE REPORT

Scene

A man sits behind a desk. There is a candle lit and a pile of papers. The man has his head buried in his hands. After a few seconds, he looks up, picks up a few pieces of paper, glances at them and then sends them flying across the table. He buries his head again. He then looks up.

Official   Who wants a job? Who wants a life?

He picks up a paper and takes it towards the candle.

Perhaps if I . . .

There is a knock at the door.

Come.

Hastily he puts the paper down. The soldier who has entered the room marches forward and stands to attention in front of the desk.

Official   You have the report?

Soldier   Yes, Sir.

Official   A complete, full, comprehensive report?

Soldier   Yes, Sir.

Official   Have the I's been dotted and the T's crossed?

Soldier   They have even been coloured in, Sir.

Official   Do we pay you to be funny?

Soldier   No, Sir; sorry, Sir. It's my weekend job as a stand-up comedian at Al's Amphitheatre Alternative Audiences.

Official   Alternative Audiences?

Soldier   Yes, Sir. If they fail to laugh . . .

The soldier gestures to show what happens by moving his finger across his throat.

Official   I think it's time to look at the report.

He begins to leaf through it.

Soldier   I think it's very funny, Sir.

Official   Funny?

Soldier   Yes, Sir. Some cracking one-liners. Great visual gags. Fantastic punchlines. I wouldn't mind lifting some of the material for my routine.

Official   This is a classified, top-secret, highly confidential document. We want to squash these reports, these rumours, this hearsay. We want to have quiet words with the witnesses. We want this all to fade away, disappear, out of sight, for ever. We do not want it broadcast by a Roman soldier in the centre of town every Saturday night. Do I make myself clear?

Soldier   Yes, Sir. Sorry, Sir.

The man shakes his head and carries on reading.

Soldier   I don't think you'll like the first report then, Sir.

Official   Why's that?

Soldier   It's hilarious!

Official   What?

Soldier   All about what happened at a wedding feast. A real rib-tickler. Had the lads in the barracks laughing for weeks!

Official   You've shown this to the lads in the barracks?

Soldier   Sir.

The man sighs and shakes his head.

Official   What can possibly be funny about a wedding feast?

Soldier   Well, Sir, it all started when . . .

Both freeze. Scene switches to centre stage.

THE FEAST

Scene

Two waiters are standing next to each other, holding pitchers of water, looking very anxious.

Waiter 1   You tell him.

Waiter 2   You tell him.

Waiter 1   No, you tell him.

Waiter 2   No, you tell him.

Waiter 1   No, you tell him.

Waiter 2   No, you tell him.

Waiter 1 points his finger in the direction of the other waiter's face.

Waiter 1   YOU tell him.

Waiter 2 removes the finger from his face, and puts his finger into Waiter 1's face.

Waiter 2   YOU tell him.

Waiter 1   I'm bigger than you.

Waiter 2   So. I have more hairs up my nose than you, but I don't go around bragging.

Waiter 1   Ugh! You disgust me!

Waiter 2   Look, you've hardly got any!

Waiter 2 ducks down and starts examining Waiter 1's nostrils. Waiter 1 puts his hand over his nose.

Waiter 1   Stop looking up my nose. You're weird, you are.

Waiter 2   I'll stop looking if you go and tell him.

Waiter 1 stands still, removes his hand, and flares his nostrils.

Waiter 1   Look as much as you want. I'm not telling him.

Waiter 2 stops looking and starts sulking.

Waiter 2   I never wanted to be a waiter. I always wanted to be a chariot driver.

Waiter 1   You think you've had it tough? I always wanted to be a Rock and Roman singer and play at the Colosseum.

He clears his throat to sing.

Waiter 2   No! You're right. We mustn't sulk. We are waiters and one of us, namely you, must go and tell him.

Waiter 1   No, you tell him.

Waiter 2   Déjà-vu.

Waiter 1   What?

Waiter 2   You never did French at school?

Waiter 1   It was all Greek to me.

Waiter 2   Never mind. Just go and tell him.

Waiter 1   No, you go and tell him.

Waiter 2   Déjà . . . No. We must stop this and do something.

Waiter 1   I know what.

Waiter 2   What?

Waiter 1   You go tell him.

Waiter 2   If you don't go and tell him, I'll pour this water over your head.

Waiter 1   If you don't go and tell him, I'll pour this water over your head and under your chin.

Mary walks onto the scene and stands next to the two waiters.

Mary   Excuse me, please, but I couldn't help noticing your . . . conversation.

The two waiters are very embarrassed.

Waiter 1   Oh.

Waiter 2   Oh.

Mary   I think you've run out of wine.

Waiter 1   Why do you say that?

Waiter 2   What on earth gave you that idea?

Both waiters hide the water behind their backs and give Mary a sickly smile.

Mary   Wasn't that water in the jar?

Waiter 1   For his hamster.

Waiter 2   For his head.

They say these lines together and stare at one another when they realise what they have said.

Waiter 1   For his hamster.

Waiter 2   Who has a bad head.

Mary   So you have run out of wine.

Both waiters nod.

Mary   And you only have water left.

Both waiters nod.

Mary   And you're worried about spoiling the whole wedding feast, telling the host, and losing your jobs.

Both nod their heads vigorously.

Mary   I'll help you. I'll go and tell him.

Mary turns to leave.

Waiter 1   Please stop.

Waiter 2   Please don't go.

Waiter 1   Don't tell him.

Waiter 2   No, don't tell him.

Waiter 1   Please don't tell him.

Waiter 2   Pretty-please don't tell him.

Mary   Oh, I'm not going to tell him.

                She looks around the room.

Mary   I'm going to tell *him*.

                Mary gives them a huge smile and then walks away.

Waiter 1   Who is that?

Waiter 2   I think it's her son.

Waiter 1   Looks like an interesting conversation.

Waiter 2   I don't care if it's fascinating, scintillating or invigorating.
                We still only have water to serve.

Waiter 1   You're right. What can he do? Turn it into wine?

                They both laugh.

Waiter 2   Now that would be something.

Waiter 1   It would be a miracle.

                They both laugh again.

Waiter 2   Oh look, he's coming over.

Waiter 1   I wonder if he's thirsty.

Waiter 2   Why, what are you going to give him? Water?

                They both laugh.
                Freeze.

FUN AT THE FEAST

Soldier   . . . and the best line was when he said, 'Why have you saved the best wine for last?'

Official   That's funny?

Soldier   Hilarious. Private Pontificus fell off his bunk laughing and smacked his body on the floor. Didn't stop him cracking up, even though he had a broken rib or two.

Official   Look at my face.

Soldier   Sir?

Official   Can you see a smile? The slightest, tiniest, faintest trace of a smile?

Soldier   I can see that smile coming, I can see that smile coming, I can see that smile coming.

The man smiles despite himself.

Soldier   Told you I could see that smile coming, Sir. My wife does that to me when I am in a sulk.

Official   I'll give you something to sulk about if you do not take this report seriously. This is a grave matter of state.

Soldier   Grave, Sir. Now that's a funny word in today's climate.

Official   I will come to that later.

He picks up the report and reads through it.

Official   Ah. What about the encounter with Nicodemus? A fine, upstanding pillar of society. No funny business here. Nothing to laugh one's sandals off about here.

Soldier   Well, Sir, now that you mention it, there was that amusing line in the middle . . .

Freeze.

NICODEMUS

Scene

Nicodemus enters. He is looking very nervous, glancing all around as he slowly walks forward.

Nicodemus   It's very dark. Very dark. I suppose it is night-time and night-times usually are dark. I don't like the dark. There could be animals out there, there could be ferocious creatures, or, even worse, tax collectors.

   Nicodemus walks slowly forward. Walking towards him is Joseph of Arimathea. They do not see each other in the dark and collide.

Nicodemus   Ow!

Joseph   Ouch!

Nicodemus   Watch where you are going!

Joseph   I can't see a thing!

Nicodemus   You've bruised my ribs.

Joseph   You nearly blinded me!

Nicodemus   I thought you couldn't see a thing?

Joseph   Nicodemus?

Nicodemus   Joseph?

   They go to hug each other and completely miss.

Nicodemus   What are you doing out here tonight?

Joseph	I'm just on my way home.
Nicodemus	Oh.
Joseph	What are you doing out here tonight?
Nicodemus	Going to meet someone.
Joseph	Who?
Nicodemus	You don't know him.
Joseph	Oh.
Nicodemus	Better be on my way. Good to see you, Joseph. Well, if I had seen you, that is.
Joseph	You too, Nicodemus. Goodnight.
Nicodemus	Goodnight.

Joseph exits.

Nicodemus My sides are aching. Imagine bumping into Joseph – literally! Still, I couldn't do this in the light, could I? What would people say? What would people think? What would happen to my career? No, it had to be tonight. It had to.

Nicodemus moves slowly and cautiously.

Nicodemus I've never met anyone like him. Never heard words like his before. Never felt like this in my whole life.

He pauses to think and reflect.

Nicodemus But what did he mean? What was he saying?

Nicodemus stops, stands still, and shakes his head, trying to understand.

Nicodemus   You must be born again.

Pause. Nicodemus turns to the audience, almost pleading with them as he raises his set of questions.

Nicodemus   You must be born again. 'How?' I asked him. How can a man be born when he is old? How can he be born from his mother's womb again? My mind was doing cartwheels. How can it be? That's when he said it. He looked into my eyes, but not just into my eyes. It felt like he was seeing straight into my soul, searching the depths of my heart.

'I tell you the truth,' he said, 'no one can enter the Kingdom of God unless he is born of water and the Spirit. Flesh gives birth to flesh, but the Spirit gives birth to spirit.'

I don't know if I understand, but I know I must. I know I need to understand. Flesh gives birth to flesh. The Spirit gives birth to spirit. You cannot enter the Kingdom unless . . . How could he say that to me? I am a religious man. I am a believer of the true faith. I keep the commandments and rules laid down by our ancestor, Moses. How can this not be enough to enter God's Kingdom? If a man like me can't enter, then who can?

Nicodemus pauses, slowly shakes his head, then looks up.

Nicodemus   It will soon be light. Maybe in the morning I will see clearly the mysteries of tonight.

Nicodemus turns to walk off stage, repeating over and over:

Nicodemus   Unless you are born again, unless you are born again, unless you are born again.

BORN AGAIN BLUES

The scene switches to the two men discussing the report.

Official   You found that amusing?

Soldier   Hysterical.

Official   One of the Jewish religious leaders absolutely baffled, confused and confounded, and all you can do is break out into a silly, cheesy grin.

Soldier   More of a belly-laugh than a cheesy grin, Sir.

Official   I know one thing.

Soldier   You do, Sir?

Official   Yes, I do.

Soldier   Sir?

Official   I am cheesed off.

Soldier   You are, Sir?

Official   No, I tell a lie. I am tickled pink. I am in the clover. I am like a lamb in the springtime. I am . . .

Soldier   You are cheesed off, aren't you, Sir?

Official   One hundred per cent.

Soldier   Is there anything I can do to cheer you up, Sir?

Official	No!
Soldier	A few jokes?
Official	No!
Soldier	Just asking, Sir.

The man holds his head and picks up the report. He reads through it.

Official	What are we going to do about this Samaritan woman's report?
Soldier	Sir?
Official	It's an incredible story.
Soldier	No one's going to listen to her, Sir.
Official	No one else is going to listen to her. Are you trying to be funny?
Soldier	No, Sir.
Official	Half the village believed because of her story.
Soldier	They did?
Official	Have you not read this?

The man slides the report across the table. The soldier picks it up and begins to read.
Freeze.

WELL, WELL, WOULD YOU BELIEVE THE WOMAN AT THE WELL?

Scene

Three women walk onto stage. They are carrying baskets full of clothes and are busy talking to each other.

Woman 1   'Come and see a man who told me everything I ever did.' That's what she said!

Woman 2   Well, I never.

Woman 3   Who wants to hear about her sordid life? How many husbands has she had?

Woman 2   I stopped counting after she got to five.

Woman 1   And that man she's living with now . . .

They all look at each other, turn away in disgust and say at the same time:

Woman 1   Ugh!

Woman 2   Ugh!

Woman 3   Ugh!

They put their fingers in their mouths to indicate their disgust.

Woman 2   I'm not saying he's ugly, but my donkey closes his eyes every time he goes past.

Woman 1   I just hold my nose.

Woman 3   She didn't just scrape the bottom of the barrel when she found him . . . He is the barrel! Have you seen the size of him?

The second woman puffs out her cheeks, holds out her arms to exaggerate how wide, how big and how fat the man is.

Woman 3   Don't do that.

Woman 2   Why not?

Woman 1   You're doing him far too much justice.

They all laugh and giggle. After a few seconds, they stop and look up.

Woman 1   Where's that crowd going?

Woman 2   No idea.

Woman 3   Why are they following her?

The women look and give disdainful expressions. On one side of the stage the Samaritan woman enters with a small crowd following her. They walk slowly off stage.

Woman 2   Because they're men.

They look at each other in disgust.

Woman 1   'Could this be the Christ?' she said.

Woman 2   Who does she think she's kidding?

Woman 3   She chats up a man at the well.

Woman 2   A Jewish bloke.

Woman 1   And tries to make out he's some holy Joe.

Woman 3   Or holy Jew.

She nudges her friends and they all giggle.

Woman 1   No one in this village is going to fall for that line. That is desperate. Why can't she admit that she was chatting him up, instead of trying to make out that he's the Messiah?

Woman 2   Just because he knows everything about her.

Woman 3   I bet everyone knows her reputation.

Woman 2   What reputation?

They nudge each other and giggle a high-pitched, hysterical laugh.

Woman 1   When that lot meet this bloke, they'll soon suss him out.

Woman 2   Soon sort him out, you mean. He's a Jew!

Woman 3   He'll wish he never sat on that well.

Woman 2   One push is all it will take!

They giggle.

Woman 1   They're coming back, look.

Woman 3   That didn't take them long.

The Samaritan woman is walking into town with a crowd of people around her. She is talking excitedly and the crowd are listening to everything she says.

Woman 1   Look at them.

Woman 2   What has she got that we haven't?

Woman 3   She's not got our good looks.

The three women start preening themselves.

Woman 1   Who's that man?

She points into the distance.

Woman 2   Don't know. Never seen him before.

Woman 3   You don't think it's . . . him?

Woman 2   Well, it's not the Messiah, is it?

They giggle again.
Freeze.

WELL, WHAT DO YOU THINK?

Soldier   You see, Sir, those women didn't believe the woman at the well.

Official   They were the only three in the village who didn't!

Soldier   But they were the village gossips, Sir. Perhaps they told lots of people not to believe her.

Official   It was too late by then. The people had met Jesus.

Soldier   Oh.

There is an awkward silence.

Official   Then there is the Official's report.

Soldier   What's this then, Sir?

Official   The official report.

Soldier   But you said there was the 'Official's report'.

Official   I meant the Official's report in the official report.

Soldier   I suppose that makes it very official. Officially official. The Official's officially official report. Have you ever noticed that when you keep on saying the same word over and over again it sounds really weird? Official. Official. Official. Official. Official.

The man gives the soldier a withering look.

Soldier   He may be an Official, but his report isn't very believable, is it? All coincidence really.

Official   Coincidence?

Soldier   Yes, Sir. You know, his son is really ill, he goes to see Jesus, Jesus says his son is healed, he meets his servants on the way home who say his son is better. 'What time did my son get better?' he asks. They tell him the time and it just so happens that it's the exact same time that Jesus says he will be healed. If that's not coincidence, Sir, I don't know what is.

The official starts to bang his head on the desk.

Soldier   Are you all right, Sir?

Official   I've felt better.

Soldier   What about that other guy, the one who really lost it.

Official   Which man?

Soldier   You know . . .

Freeze.

SEE HOW THEY LEAP

Scene
A man leaps on to the stage, punching the air in triumph.

Man   Yes! Yes! Yes!

He jumps for joy.

Man   Yes!

In one hand he is clutching a mat. He throws it into the air and catches it.

Man   Yes!

He jumps up and down on the spot, laughing and shouting for joy. Suddenly he stops, stands still, and looks up.

Man   Thank you.

He falls on his knees, looks down, bows his head.

Man   Thank you.

He holds his legs. After a few seconds, he stands up, picks up his mat and starts walking. A Pharisee walks on to stage, sees the man and looks horrified.

Pharisee   Halt!

The man stops.

Pharisee   Where do you think you are going?

Man   I was just walking.

Pharisee	Walking?
Man	Yeah, and before that I was kneeling, before that I was jumping. Oh and leaping – don't forget leaping.
Pharisee	You are carrying your mat.
Man	Yeah. Yeah, I am. I'm not sitting on it, or lying on it. I am carrying it.

He throws the mat in the air and dances around. Starts to sing like a children's rhyme:

Man	I'm carrying my mat, I'm carrying my mat, I'm carrying my mat.
Pharisee	It is the Sabbath! The law forbids you to carry your mat.
Man	The man who made me well said, 'Pick up your mat', so I thought if I can stand up I'm picking up my mat.
Pharisee	And now you're breaking the law.
Man	Who made the law?
Pharisee	How dare you question me!
Man	Just asking. Now if you don't know . . .
Pharisee	God. God made the law.
Man	And your next question for ten bonus points. Who alone can heal people?

The Pharisee stands, fuming.

Man	It's not a difficult question, not too tricky, not trying to catch you out.

There is an awkward silence.

Man   I'll give you a clue.

Leaning to whisper the clue to the Pharisee.

Man   It's the same answer as the last question.

Pharisee   I know that. Of course I know that.

Man   Yeah, course you did. So why didn't you say so?

Pharisee   Because . . .

Man   Yeah?

Pharisee   Because . . .

Man   Yeah?

Pharisee   Because . . .

Man   You don't know, do you?

Pharisee   I don't know who told you to pick up your mat and walk
                on the Sabbath. No, I don't. Who is he?

*The man who has been healed starts to speak and then stops
to think.*

Man   He was . . .

Pharisee   Yes?

Man   He was . . .

Pharisee   I'm waiting.

Man   He was . . .

Pharisee   I'm still wondering.

Man   He was . . . here a moment ago. He must have slipped into the crowd. It can't be too difficult to find him. How many people do you know who can make cripples walk?

Pharisee   Not on the Sabbath, I know that much.

Man   That's funny. I thought God could heal whenever he wants.

Pharisee   This is not funny. You don't see me laughing, my lips grinning, or my face twitching with amusement, do you?

The man examines his face.

Man   No, I don't. But it looks like you could do with a good laugh. When was the last time you had your ribs tickled?

Starts prodding the Pharisee in the ribs.

Pharisee   I could have you arrested!

Man   You'd have to catch me first!

The man runs away.
Freeze.

WHAT'S THE MATTER WITH YOU?

Soldier   What a nutter, Sir.

Official   Nutter?

Soldier   One pillar short of a temple, he was, Sir.

Official   You'll be saying he'd lost his marbled stones next.

Soldier   Well, he nearly lost his mat!

Official   His mat?

Soldier   Yes, Sir. Throwing it into the air like that. That's no way to treat a mat, is it Sir? I bought a brand-new one for the house the other day. Takes pride of place it does. If my missus caught me sending it into orbit, she'd think I was from another planet.

Official   Did you stop to think why he might be throwing his mat in the air?

Soldier   I'd rather not, Sir.

Official   You'd rather not?

Soldier   No, Sir, if you don't mind.

Official   And why don't you want to think about it, might I ask?

Soldier   Too upsetting, Sir.

Official   Too upsetting?

The soldier explains himself, getting more and more upset as he goes on.

Soldier   Yes, Sir. Someone throwing a poor, innocent, helpless mat around like that. They deserve to be locked up. Especially after all the good years of service that mat had provided. Laying on it, sprawled on it day by day, year after year. You'd think he would have thought about that mat a little bit more instead of throwing it around.

Official   Well, yes, but the man obviously wasn't too concerned about that. He could walk! People would call that a miracle. But I can't write that in my report, can I? 'Jesus the miracle worker'. They would throw me out of the service. No. What we need to do is think carefully about all this and concoct a story that is credible. Nothing miraculous. We need to use our loaf.

Soldier   That's what Jesus did, Sir.

Official   What?

Soldier   Used his loaf.

Official   His brain?

Soldier   No, Sir, bread! The loaf of bread. You know, Sir, it's in the report . . .

The man looks at the report.
Freeze.

PREQUEL TO
'USING YOUR LOAF'

Man   Didn't.

Woman   Did.

Man   Didn't.

Woman   Did.

Man   Didn't.

Woman   Did.

Man   You always think you're right.

Woman   Only because you're always wrong.

Man   There are no shops nearby.

The woman starts clapping.

Man   What are you doing?

Woman   Clapping.

Man   I know that! But why?

Woman   Because you have just got something right.

Man   You see, I told you I was right.

Woman   No, you're wrong.

Man   You just said I was right.

Woman   About the shops, not about the food.

Man   If there were no shops, there could be no food, not for that crowd. No way did he do it, no way.

The man folds his arms defiantly and stands his ground. The woman shakes her head and walks away. Before she leaves the stage she turns round.

Woman   Did!

The man looks very cross, unfolds his arms and shouts.

Man   Didn't!

The woman is now off-stage but you hear her shout.

Woman   Did!

The man charges after her and off-stage you hear them shouting, 'Did' and 'Didn't'. They grow quieter and quieter as Harry and Larry walk onto the stage.

USING YOUR LOAF

Scene

A man is tearing up a piece of paper. He throws it on the ground, and jumps up and down on it. Along comes his friend who stands and watches him. When the man finishes jumping on the paper, his friend speaks to him.

Larry You upset, Harry?

Harry No, Larry. I'm happy. Can't you tell?

Larry No, Harry. Looks like you're upset, stomping around like that.

Harry No, Larry, I was jumping for joy.

Larry Oh, Harry, I thought you looked a trifle tantrum-ish.

Harry No, Larry. Why would I be throwing a wobbler? Why should I be manically depressed? What on earth have I got to be sick as a pig about?

Larry 'Parrot' ain't it, Harry? 'Sick as a parrot'.

    Starting to sound threatening.

Harry Since when have you seen a parrot in Palestine, Larry?

Larry Pig. Pig. Pig. Pig. Pig, Harry, pig.

Harry Who's a pig, Larry? Who's a pig?

Larry Not you, Harry, not you.

Harry Life's a pig, Larry, that's what. Life's a pig . . .

    Harry breaks down and begins to sob.

Larry	You upset, Harry?
Harry	No, Larry, I always cry when I'm happy.
Larry	Same as my missus, Harry. She cries when she's happy.
Harry	Ever heard of sarcasm, Larry?
Larry	No, Harry. Is it near Samaria?
Harry	Larry, let me spell it out for you.
Larry	Why, Harry, is it a long word?
Harry	Do you want to understand what I am on about or not, Larry?
Larry	That would be a first, Harry.
Harry	Are you trying to be funny, Larry?
Larry	Not to the best of my knowledge, Harry.
Harry	Larry, are you going to listen to me, or are you going to keep jabbering on like a jibber?
Larry	I'm listening, Harry, I'm listening.
Harry	Good, Larry, 'cos my story is . . .
Larry	What's a jibber jabber Harry?
Harry	Have you completely lost the plot, Larry?
Larry	Sorry, Harry, I didn't even know you'd started the story.
Harry	Larry . . .

Larry	Yes, Harry?
Harry	Shut up, Larry.
Larry	Yes, Harry.
Harry	You know that geezer Jesus, Larry?

Larry says nothing.

Harry	You know, the one who was feeding the crowd the other day.

Still Larry says nothing.

Harry	You must know, Larry. It's the talk of the whole town. He fed thousands of people with just a few loaves and a couple of fish. Thousands, Larry. Not just one or two, or ten or twenty or two hundred, but thousands. So I thought to myself, this is going to be a nice little earner, Harry-boy. So I went straight out I did and bought the bakery. All I had to do was ask Jesus to 'bless' my bread, and Harry-boy was going to be a very rich man, a *very* rich man. You get my drift, Harry? Larry, you can speak . . . LARRY!!!
Larry	Yes, Harry. Sorry, Harry. Shut up, Larry; speak up, Larry; whatever you say, Harry.
Harry	Larry . . .
Larry	Yes, Harry?
Harry	Shut up, Larry.
Larry	Yes, Harry.
Harry	Where was I? Oh yes. Well, today I go along to meet this

THE WORD THAT CHANGED THE WORLD

guy Jesus, and tell him the good news about my bakery. Only thing is, as I get near him I hear him telling the crowd, 'Do no work for food that spoils, but for food that endures for eternal life.' But that's not all, Larry-boy. He also says 'The bread of God is he who comes down from heaven and gives life to the world.'

Larry   What kind of bread's that, Harry? I mean, I've had lots of tasty bread but nothing I would say tasted like heaven. What does heaven taste like, Harry?

Harry   Larry, this bloke didn't talk about *bread* bread. He said, 'I am the bread of life. He who comes to me will never go hungry, and he who believes in me will never be thirsty.'

Larry   So he's giving out free drinks as well, is he, Harry?

Harry   He was talking about himself, Larry. Now what am I going to do? Who on earth can I sell the bakery to now? It's no good to me. It is useless. Which idi . . . Larry?

Larry   Yes, Harry.

Harry   You like baking?

Larry   Yes, Harry.

The two men walk off, Harry with his arm around Larry's shoulder, trying to convince him to buy the bakery.

WHOLESOME WHOLEMEAL

Soldier   A few slices short of a loaf, that Larry, if you ask me, Sir.

Official   I am not asking you anything. I am thinking.

Soldier   Yes, Sir. Sir?

Official   What?

Soldier   You wouldn't have bought the bakery, would you, Sir?

Official   Of course not!

Soldier   Just checking, Sir. Sir?

Official   What now?

Soldier   What are you thinking about, if it's not the bakery?

Official   Believe it or not, I am thinking about this report, and what I am going to report back to Rome.

Soldier   There's no place like Rome, is there, Sir? No place like Rome. No place like home. Hey – that rhymes! I might use that in my act. No place like Rome. No place like home. What do you think, Sir?

The man gives him a withering look.

Soldier   I'll be quiet, shall I, Sir?

Another glaring look from the man.

Soldier   Yes, I'll be quiet then, Sir.

Official   I can't think what to do in this situation.

Soldier   Just like that blind man, Sir.

Official   What blind man?

Soldier   The blind man who couldn't see until he could see, if you see what I mean, Sir.

Official   No, I don't see.

Soldier   It's in the report, Sir. Why don't you look and see?

Freeze.

NOW DO YOU SEE?

Scene
A man is standing in the dock. A Pharisee is prowling the courtroom.

Man Boo! *(This is said in a very dramatic fashion)*

He removes his hands from in front of his face as he says 'Boo'. The Pharisee glares at him.

Pharisee Not funny.

Man Boo!

Pharisee Will you stop doing that?

Man Boo!

Pharisee If you don't stop being so silly, you will be removed from this courtroom. Do I make myself clear?

Man Spoil-sport.

Pharisee You are here to answer the charges, not to charge around court playing childish games.

Man Can't I play 'I spy' again?

Pharisee No!

Man But it's such good fun.

Pharisee Not for me, it's not.

Man But there is so much I can see!

Pharisee I wish you could see that I am extremely annoyed with your childish antics.

Man	I can't see why.
Pharisee	You can't see at all, that's your problem.
Man	Oh, but I can see! I can see everything clearly, and that's your problem.

The Pharisee takes a deep sigh.

Pharisee	You say that this man is a Prophet.
Man	He is – look at my eyes!
Pharisee	We know this man is a sinner.
Man	Whether he is a sinner or not, I don't know. One thing I do know – I was blind, but now I can see.
Pharisee	What did he do to you? How did he open your eyes?
Man	I've told you already and you didn't listen. Why do you want to hear it again? Do you want to become his disciples too?
Pharisee	Wash your mouth out! Who do you think you are talking to? What gives you the right to tell us anything? We know that you were born in sin, steeped in sin at birth. We, however, are disciples of Moses. You, on the other hand, are a disciple of this fellow. We know that God spoke to Moses, but as for this fellow, we don't even know where he comes from.
Man	Now that is remarkable! You don't know where he comes from, yet he opened my eyes. We know that God does not listen to sinners. He listens to the godly man who does his will. Nobody has ever heard of opening the eyes of a man born blind. If this man were not from God, he could do nothing.

Pharisee How dare you lecture us? How dare you stand and speak to us in such language? How dare you darken our Synagogue with your presence? How dare you?

Man It is true, what they say.

Pharisee What venomous lies are you going to bombard us with now?

Man No one is blinder than he who will not see.

Pharisee Out! Out! Out! Before we throw you out of this place! Out! Do not dare set one toe across the threshold of this temple. You are banished!

The man walks slowly to the door. He pauses, then turns around.

Man I had hoped . . . you might have rejoiced with me. My joy, God's glory, sight restored, healing of the body, but I see that you need a deeper healing than me. You need your stone hearts turning into flesh.

Pharisee Out!

Man I know that he could do it.

Pharisee Out!!

Man If you'd only let him.

Pharisee OUT!!

The man exits.

TO DIE FOR

Official   The blind man doesn't help me to see what to do.

Soldier   Ex-blind man, Sir.

Official   OK, the ex-blind man.

Soldier   That's right, Sir.

Official   And there is no evidence to suggest that any of these witnesses will retract their statements.

Soldier   We can ensure their silence, Sir.

Official   We can? How?

Soldier   Kill them.

Official   Kill them?

Soldier   Yes, Sir.

Official   Kill them all?

Soldier   Yes, Sir.

Official   Have you any idea just how many people met Jesus?

Soldier   I know – it will keep the lads on overtime for a good few months.

Official   I think you are missing the point.

Soldier   Am I, Sir?

Official   Yes. Just a little bit. We cannot go around the country killing people who say things we don't like.

Soldier   Since when, Sir?

Official   Since I was in charge around here.

Soldier   Oh. Things have changed then, have they, Sir?

Official   We will only stir up the nation by slaughtering the innocent. Didn't you learn anything in your history lessons at school?

Soldier   Only how many countries we've conquered and how many people we've killed. I'm red-hot on those stats, Sir. Go on, test me.

Official   I don't think I have the time or the inclination for some reason. Ah, let me see . . . here's the reason: I AM TRYING TO RULE THIS PROVINCE AND PUT DOWN THIS SECT, THE SO-CALLED 'FOLLOWERS OF THE WAY'. I think that is keeping me a little preoccupied at the moment.

Soldier   Yes, Sir. Sorry, Sir.

Official   Let me look at the next report. Errm – oh yes. Two sisters. They sound very nice and friendly, good at making meals for people. Very harmless.

Soldier   I don't think you want to read that report, Sir.

Official   Because their brother died? Hmm, rather sad, I do admit.

Soldier   It's the bit over the page I wouldn't read, Sir . . .

Freeze.

NOTHING SO GRAVE

Scene
Mary and Martha are rushing around the house, busy preparing.

Mary	I'll cook tonight.
Martha	You?
Mary	Yes.
Martha	Cook?
Mary	That's what I said.
Martha	Are you sure?
Mary	I'm offering.
Martha	I'm accepting.
Mary	Good.
Martha	Good.

Martha goes to the bottom of the stairs and shouts up.

Martha	Are you awake yet?
Mary	Sshh – he's having a rest.
Martha	He's been lying down for the last few days. You'd think he'd want to be up and about by now.
Mary	I think it's taken a lot out of him.
Martha	It's taken a lot out of me, but I'm still keeping going.

Mary   I know, but you're different.

Martha   What do you mean, I'm different?

Mary   He's a man.

Martha   Oh yeah.

Mary   I think he'll be all right once he's had a rest.

Martha   Yeah, I'm sure you're right.

Mary   How many are we expecting tonight?

Martha   It could be the whole village.

Mary   You're kidding!

Martha   I never joke where food's concerned.

Mary   But we can't cater for crowds!

Martha   They may not all come.

Mary   I think a load of them went straight off, celebrating.

Martha   It might just be a few of us tonight, then.

Mary   I hope so.

Martha   So do I.

Mary   It's been such a . . . such a . . . such a few days. I just want a quiet meal.

Martha   With a few friends.

Mary   Yeah, and relax, enjoying each other's company and just . . . just enjoy.

Mary and Martha smile at each other.

Martha   Can you believe it?

Mary   No.

Martha   I still think I'm dreaming.

Mary   I don't want to wake up if I am.

Martha   It's not a dream, is it?

Mary   No.

Martha   No, it's not. It's all too real, too incredible, too unbeliev-
               able but real, definitely real.

Mary   Is this really happening to us?

Martha   Yeah.

Mary   I feel like laughing.

Martha   I feel like crying.

Mary   I feel like dancing.

Martha   I feel like weeping.

Mary   I feel so alive!

Martha   I felt like I was so dead.

They look at each other and laugh.

Mary   Like our brother.

Martha   Good old Lazarus.

Mary	He was dead, Martha.
Martha	I know.
Mary	He was in the tomb for days.
Martha	I know.
Mary	He did look funny.
Martha	What?
Mary	Walking about in his grave clothes.
Martha	I don't think he expected to be walking anywhere. Did you?
Mary	No. And you thought he'd stink rotten!
Martha	He had been in the tomb for four days.
Mary	I know – four days!
Martha	Four whole days!!
Mary	Did you see the look on his face?
Martha	I'll never forget it.
Mary	When he saw Jesus.
Martha	I thought he was going to pass out.
Mary	You could say he was somewhat amazed.
Martha	We'll never be the same, will we, Mary?
Mary	No. No, we won't.

The two sisters stare at each other.

Martha   Lazarus!

Mary   Lazarus!

Martha   It's a good job he responded quicker to Jesus!

They say together

Mary   Lazarus!

Martha   Lazarus!

Freeze.

YOU CAN'T KEEP A GOOD MAN DOWN

Official   This report could finish me off.

Soldier   Just look at Lazarus, Sir. He thought he was finished, but he made a comeback!

Official   It's stories like Lazarus's that will bury my career. Do you understand?

Soldier   Yes, Sir.

Official   What can I say about this incident?

Soldier   Nothing, Sir.

Official   Nothing?

Soldier   Yes, Sir. Say nothing. Pretend it never happened. You don't tell anyone, I won't tell anyone.

Official   That's a good idea.

Soldier   Thank you, Sir.

Official   We don't mention it to anyone.

Soldier   No, Sir.

Official   We'll act like it never happened.

Soldier   Yes, Sir.

Official   Oh dear.

Soldier   What's wrong, Sir?

Official   Oh, just all the people who were eye-witnesses who will talk about nothing else for the rest of their lives.

Soldier   We could . . .

Official   No we could not kill them all!

Soldier   Just an idea, Sir.

Official   Not a good one. Besides, killing people doesn't guarantee that they stay dead!

Soldier   No, Sir.

Official   Look at Lazarus.

Soldier   Precisely. He couldn't stay dead for more than four days.

Official   Exactly.

Soldier   We could circulate stories about how all of Jesus' friends were nutters.

Official   Nutters?

Soldier   Yes, Sir, nutters. Like the woman who dried his feet with her hair. She was a nutter, Sir. Real fruitcake. Barmy as a bat. Lost the plot, didn't even know what day it was. Cuckoo, she was Sir. Loopy Loo.

Official   Shut up! Before you drive me crazy. Let me read the report.

Freeze.

SAVING UP TO SACRIFICE

Scene

A crowded shop. It is the best place in town, with the finest, top of the range, goods. People are busy browsing and buying. Shop workers are busy attending to their customers. There is a lot of activity and a low level of noise as people talk and chatter.

The door opens and in walks a woman of low reputation. There is instant silence as she enters the shop. Everyone stops and stares. As she begins to move around the shop people make a quick exit, leaving the two shop assistants arguing about who is going to serve her.

Shop Assistant 1 = SA1
Shop Assistant 2 = SA2

SA1	You go.
SA2	No. You go.
SA1	I'm not talking to her.
SA2	I can't even look at her.
SA1	We could throw her out.
SA2	I'm not going anywhere near her.
SA1	Someone has to serve her.
SA2	Not if they can't see her.

On saying this he closes his eyes and wanders around the shop. The woman sees him and stares in disbelief. The manager of the shop has been watching everything and steps in to sort things out.

Manager — Take your friend into the back of the shop. I will speak to you both later!

He says this in a low growl in the ear of Shop Assistant 2 then turns to the woman and puts on a huge false smile.

Manager   Ah, Madam, how may I help you? Are you lost?

Woman   No.

Manager   Oh! I thought you might have stepped into the wrong shop.

Woman   No.

He smiles a false smile.

Manager   If you are waiting for someone can I ask you to wait outside.

Woman   I've come to buy something.

The man almost chokes.

Manager   From this shop?

Woman   That would be a good reason for being here.

Manager   But . . . but . . . but . . . but . . . but . . .

Woman   But what?

Manager   The prices!

Woman   . . . are very expensive.

Manager   Yes. I don't mean to be rude, Madam, but there is not a solitary item in this shop that you could purchase.

The two shop assistants have now re-emerged and are listening to the conversation. They nod in full agreement with the manager's words.

SA1	Shoo!
SA2	Shoo!

The manager turns around and gives them an angry look. The two shop assistants start to cough and look around the shop to avoid eye contact with the manager.

Woman	What about that?

She points to an item. The manager looks and laughs.

Manager	Madam, you have a good sense of humour.
Woman	How much?

The manager stops laughing.

Manager	That would cost a year's wages.

The woman pauses to think.

Woman	I'll buy it.

She goes to get her money. The manager faints. The two shop assistants rush over to try to revive him.

Freeze.

SACRIFICIAL SCENT

Soldier   See what I mean, Sir. Spending a whole year's wages on a jar of perfume. I don't let my wife spend a cent on scent. Waste of money.

Official   Yes, I had noticed your wife's . . . aroma.

Soldier   The woman was off her trolley, out of her mind, on another planet, in La La Land.

Official   Thank you, soldier. I get the picture, I don't need you to keep colouring it in.

Soldier   A complete balm pot!

Official   Soldier!

Soldier   Yes, Sir.

Official   Some people may look upon her act as one of supreme sacrifice. Giving all she had on one item.

Soldier   That's not sacrifice, Sir, that's stupidity. A sacrifice is when you lay down your life for your empire, standing on the front line, facing the enemy.

Official   Yes, that is sacrifice.

The official looks at the report.

Soldier   Sir, what are you reading?

The official looks up.

Official   It's the report of the crucifixion.

Soldier   Ah.

Official   You were there. You remember what happened?

Soldier   Yes, Sir. It's all written down.

Song: Tonight

TONIGHT

For song words and music see page 82.

Mary and John walk slowly to centre stage. They stand looking forward as the song is sung. John comforts Mary as they look at the cross. The stage lighting needs to be soft lights on Mary and John and begin turning to a red light to show Jesus' death and then complete darkness as Mary and John leave the stage.

Or alternatively . . .

THE CROSS

The stage is set in darkness. Two forlorn figures move slowly to the centre. It's Mary and John. As they stand looking forward there is the sound of a hammer hitting a nail. There is a pause between each blow. John puts his arm around Mary who buries her head into John's chest, unable to look. After a number of hammer-blows there is absolute silence. Mary turns to look at the cross. John and Mary hold their positions for a while; there is the sound of thunder before John leads Mary away.

Stage Directions: A soft light on Mary and John would work well. If possible the white light turning to red after the sound of the hammer to depict Jesus' death. At the sound of the thunderclap the stage falls into darkness. The sound of the hammer and nail and the thunderclap would probably work best on tape coming over the PA. The scene needs to be played slowly to allow for the dramatic tension and drama that is unfolding.

THE END OF THE ROAD, OR JUST A CROSSROADS?

Scene

Two men walk silently across stage. Their heads are bowed, their bodies slumped. They walk on. Joseph sits on the floor, Nicodemus prefers to stand. Mary is already sitting there.

Joseph   Do you want to talk?

Mary shakes her head.

Joseph   I need to talk.

Nicodemus It's a free world.

Joseph   I just don't know what to say.

Nicodemus What can you say?

Joseph   I don't know.

Nicodemus How can anyone say anything? How can anyone make any sense of this?

He gestures behind him. Joseph holds his head in his hands and rubs his eyes.

Joseph   I wish I'd spoken up.

Nicodemus Would it have made any difference?

Joseph   I don't know.

Nicodemus says very quietly:

Nicodemus No one spoke up.

Joseph I could have tried. I could have said something, done something.

Nicodemus What?

Joseph I don't know.

Joseph stands up at this point. He is angry with what has happened and with himself.

Nicodemus Overturned the decision?

Joseph No.

Nicodemus Out-shouted the crowd?

Joseph No.

Nicodemus Over-run the soldiers?

Joseph No.

Nicodemus So what could you have done?

Joseph I could have been there for him. Done something. Said something. Showed him that . . .

Nicodemus Showed him what?

There is a pause.

Joseph That I cared.

Nicodemus I know.

Joseph But did he know?

Another pause.

Mary   He knows.

Mary stands up and puts a hand on Joseph's arm. Both men look away into the distance.

Nicodemus   He seemed to know everything, have all the answers and the questions. He set my mind puzzling for weeks: 'You must be born again.'

Nicodemus smiles at the recollection.

Joseph   I feel like I only understood him when it was too late.

Nicodemus   I know.

Mary   I think I always understood *(she smiles)*. There are some things I've known, things I've treasured all my life.

She smiles at the memories, then wipes a tear away.

Joseph   I thought the people knew him too. His entry into Jerusalem. The reaction of the crowds, the praises, the adoration, the worship. I thought, I really thought this was it, the Messiah. I dared to believe in him. I thought I saw something in him that was different.

Mary   You did.

The two men look at each other.

Joseph   So why?

Nicodemus tries to answer but cannot find the words.

Nicodemus   I don't know, Joseph, I just don't know.

Pause.

Joseph   Did you see his face, when he was on the cross?

Nicodemus   Yes.

Joseph   Even though he was bruised, beaten, bloody, there was something about his face. Do you know what I mean?

Mary   There was love. Always love.

Joseph   There was a peace too. Not just an acceptance of death, but something else behind those eyes.

Nicodemus   I saw his eyes.

There is a pause.

Joseph   'Forgive them,' he said.

Nicodemus   How could he?

Joseph   I don't know.

Nicodemus   But he said it.

Joseph   And meant it.

Nicodemus   I know. I know.

Joseph   Did you stay to the end?

Nicodemus   Yes.

Joseph   Did you hear his final words?

Nicodemus   Yes.

A pause.

Joseph   'It is finished.'

Nicodemus   Then he bowed his head.

Joseph   'It is finished.' Words to say it was over, the race run, his life ending.

Nicodemus   Is that how you saw it?

Joseph   How else can you see it? We just buried him.

Nicodemus   I know. I know. But there was something in his eyes, in his voice.

Joseph   What?

Nicodemus   I don't know. Maybe it's just me, the day, everything. Oh, I don't know.

Joseph   No, go on. How did you see it? What did you hear?

Pause.

Nicodemus   A beginning.

Mary stands and smiles. She is tired and weary but carries a treasured hope in her heart.

Mary   Come on, it's late. I'm going home now. I need to rest, I need to be up early in the morning.

Freeze.

THE END?

SACRIFICE OR NOT?

Official	Nothing wrong with that report.
Soldier	No, Sir.
Official	Jesus was dead.
Soldier	Yes, Sir.
Official	We Romans don't mess about.
Soldier	No, Sir.
Official	We take care of our business.
Soldier	Yes, Sir.
Official	Efficiency.
Soldier	Sir?
Official	—That's how we run our empire. Efficiency. Efficiency, economy, and . . . everything else which is good about being a Roman.
Soldier	Yes, Sir.
Official	We don't crucify people for nothing.
Soldier	No, Sir. It's usually when people have committed a crime.
Official	Yes, well, in most cases that's true. There are always exceptions to rules, aren't there?

Soldier   Yes, Sir.

Official   Makes life more efficient.

Soldier   Yes, Sir.

Official   Tidy up loose ends. Make everything nice and neat, keep the wheels of the empire running smoothly.

Soldier   Clickety-clack. Clickety-clack.

Official   What?

Soldier   Chariots, Sir. Clickety-clack. Clickety-clack. That's what they sound like when they are running smoothly. Clickety-clack. Clickety-clack.

Official   You ever been run over by a chariot, soldier?

Soldier   No, Sir.

Official   You want it to stay that way?

Soldier   Yes, Sir.

Official   Then SHUT UP!

Soldier   Sir!

Official   Efficiency. That's my motto. Efficiency.

Soldier   I thought that mottoes had more than one word, Sir.

Official   I thought we agreed that you were being silent.

Soldier   Sorry, Sir.

Official   How come there are more pages left in the report? That's not efficient, is it? Bad waste of paper if you ask me. Not very efficient at all.

Soldier   Well, Sir. There's a reason for more paper.

Official   There'd better be a good reason.

Soldier   You may not want to read it, Sir.

Official   Of course I do. It wouldn't be efficient if I didn't.

Freeze.

FAILURES, FISH AND FORGIVENESS

Scene
Two people are standing watching Peter on the beach.

James   Look at him.

Salome   I know.

Peter is wandering up and down the beach.

James   What do you think's got into him?

Salome   You don't think he's going to try walking on water again?

James   No!

Salome   Perhaps it's the conversation he's had.

James   No!

Pauses.

James   Oh yeah.

Salome looks and nods.

Salome   Something's going through his mind.

James   It's OK. Look, John will sort him out.

John   Peter, why are you counting the fish?

Peter   I'm hyperactive. I always have been.

John	But you've counted them three times already.
Peter	I told you, I'm hyperactive. I need to do something.
John	Well, how many fish did we catch?
Peter	I don't know, I keep forgetting.
John	It doesn't matter.
Peter	Yes it does. I'll count them again.
John	Please don't. You don't have to.
Peter	But I want to.
John	It's not important.
Peter	I want to count!
John	We don't need an exact figure.
Peter	I love counting!
John	We . . . can't wait to find out how many.
Peter	Good.

Peter digs into the net and begins counting. After a while he stops.

John	Do you want a hand?
Peter	What?
John	You've stopped counting.
Peter	I know.

John	I wondered if you'd run out of fingers and thumbs.
Peter	Very funny.
John	Thank you.
Peter	I can't count now. I can't concentrate.
John	I'm not surprised.

Peter looks at John.

Peter	Can you believe it?
John	What? That you've stopped counting, you're standing still, and not doing anything?
Peter	No, not that.
John	Only kidding.
Peter	Very funny.
John	Thank you.
Peter	You know what I'm talking about, don't you?
John	I think so.
Peter	This time I really thought I'd blown it.
John	We all did.
Peter	I know we all ran, John, but I was the only one who denied knowing him.
John	Peter . . .

Peter	You don't have to say anything, John.
John	I don't know what to say.
Peter	Neither did I. At first when I saw him again, I couldn't believe it, I hardly dared hope.
John	We all felt the same.
Peter	But you didn't have my shame.
John	I'm sorry.
Peter	So was I. More than I could express. Even me, Peter. I was speechless.

There is a pause.

John	But Jesus spoke to you.
Peter	Yes, he did.
John	And . . . I don't mean to pry, Peter . . .
Peter	No, it's OK. I want to share. Do you know what he asked me?
John	No.
Peter	'Do you love me?' That's what he said. Can you imagine how I felt? What I thought? Of course I love him. More than life. I had wept bitter tears after my denial, I had cried myself to sleep over his death. I had mourned and gone without food because of my sadness. Of course I love him.
John	Did you tell him?

Peter	I think he knew. I'm sure he knew, but I told him. Yes, I told him.
John	What did he say?
Peter	He said, 'Feed my sheep.' Then he asked me again if I loved him.
John	Again?
Peter	He asked me three times.
John	Three?
Peter	I think I know why . . . And three times he told me to feed his sheep, take care of his lambs. John . . . he's forgiven me, he loves me, he has a job for me, for me!
John	Peter, I'm so happy. I'm so pleased for you. It's great. It's more than great, it's brilliant. What can I say?
Peter	That you'd like to count the fish for me?
John	What?
Peter	I'm too excited to count. You don't mind, do you, mate?
John	One, two, three . . .

BUT IT WON'T LAST OR
FAMOUS LAST WORDS

Official   They were two of his disciples.

Soldier   Yes, Sir.

Official   Talking about the man they had been following.

Soldier   Yes, Sir.

Official   That's quite natural, quite normal behaviour – remembering their leader.

Soldier   In the present tense, Sir?

Official   Present?

Soldier   After his crucifixion.

Official   When he had been killed.

Soldier   Yes, Sir.

Official   This doesn't make sense.

Soldier   No, Sir.

Official   Dead men don't walk.

Soldier   No, Sir.

Official   Dead men don't talk.

Soldier   No, Sir.

Official   Dead men don't cook.

Soldier   No, Sir.

Official   Dead men don't eat fish.

Soldier   No, Sir, but people who are alive do.

Official   Alive?

Soldier   That's what the disciples say.

Official   Deluded, demented disciples is what I say.

Soldier   And all the thousands of people who've recently become converts. I have another rather thick file I could show you. Eye-witness accounts, testimonies, people who've been imprisoned but still say Jesus is alive. I could bring you the file . . .

Official   Burn it.

Soldier   Burn it, Sir?

Official   We don't need to tell Rome about this.

Soldier   No, Sir.

Official   It's not as if these rumours will ever reach Rome, is it?

Soldier   No, Sir.

Official   All this fuss will die down in a few weeks.

Soldier   Yes, Sir.

Official   A couple of months at the most.

Soldier   Yes, Sir.

Official   This time next year it will all be forgotten.

Soldier   Yes, Sir. And a thousand years from now no one will even remember his name.

Official   Whose name?

Soldier   Very good, Sir. Very funny.

Official   No, I'm convinced that this will all blow over.

Official stands up, walks away from his desk, pauses before the next line which is delivered in an emphatic tone.

Official   Dead men don't change the world.

Soldier   No, Sir. Dead men don't change the world.

Soldier says this with a question in his voice. Both look at each other. There are questions in their minds. They look away, to the audience, their faces showing that Jesus may well be . . . alive.

Freeze.

Song: Alpha and Omega (see page 85).

APPENDIX

WORDS AND MUSIC

TONIGHT

(See pages 63 and 84)

1. To - night, when the world rests on your shoul - ders, oh, to - night, a
2. day, when your dreams are liv - ing night - mares, oh, to - day, does

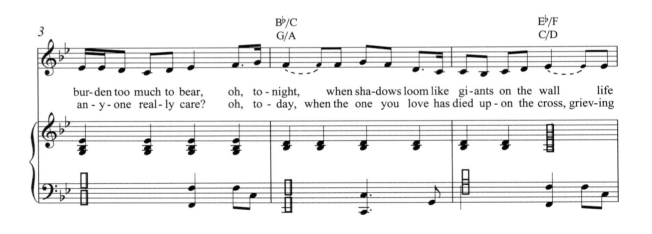

bur - den too much to bear, oh, to - night, when sha - dows loom like gi - ants on the wall life
an - y - one real - ly care? oh, to - day, when the one you love has died up - on the cross, griev - ing

makes no sense at all. But like an o - a - sis,
hearts, the pain the loss.

Refrain

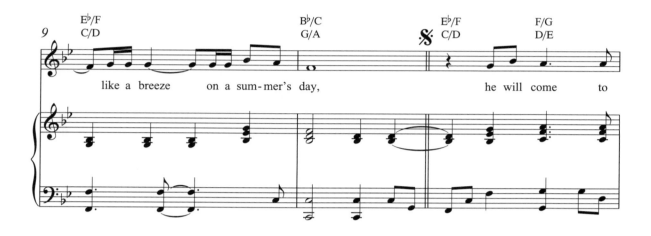

like a breeze on a sum-mer's day, he will come to

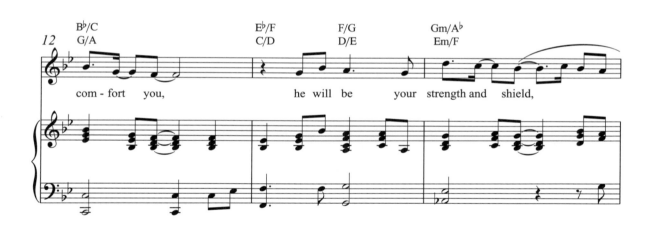

com - fort you, he will be your strength and shield,

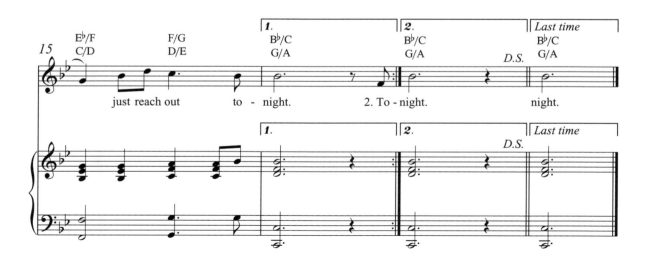

just reach out to - night. 2. To - night. night.

TONIGHT

Tonight, when the world rests on your shoulders,
oh, tonight, a burden too much to bear,
oh, tonight, when shadows loom like giants on the wall
life makes no sense at all.

But like an oasis,
like a breeze on a summer's day,
he will come to comfort you,
he will be your strength and shield,
just reach out tonight.

Today, when your dreams are living nightmares,
oh, today, does anyone really care?
oh, today, when the one you love has died upon the cross,
grieving hearts, the pain the loss.

But like an oasis,
like a breeze on a summer's day,
he will come to comfort you,
he will be your strength and shield,
just reach out tonight.

He will come to comfort you,
he will be your strength and shield,
just reach out tonight.

ALPHA AND OMEGA

(See pages 79 and 86)

ALPHA AND OMEGA

Alpha and Omega;
Jesus, King and friend.
Alpha and Omega:
the beginning and the end.

He is the Shepherd of our souls,
he is the Saviour of us all.

Chorus

He is the rock on which we stand,
he is the hope for all the land.

Chorus

He is the light by which we see,
he is the one to set us free.

Chorus

He is Redeemer of mankind,
he is the treasure we can find.

Chorus
(repeated twice, last line repeated again to finish)